NIGHT TIME

Night Time
By
Sara DeGraff

Night Time
Published and copyrighted by
Timeless Avatar Press
ISBN *0-9733692-1-3*
All rights reserved. No part of this book may be used or reproduced in any manner whatsoever without written permission

The author wishes to thank George Elliot Clarke, Anna Jean Mallinson, Ronald Big and lenore Stoneberg for their support.

Night Time •5

*My greatest view of the universe
Has been under the darkest sky*

6 • Sara DeGraff

Dark are the days of my life,
Dark are the nights of my life,
So dark that time has slipped me by.

Night Time •7

*I live in a distant past
Where most of my todays
Have gone untouched,
And turned into empty memories.*

*For a long time,
I felt my life force
Disintegrating right before my eyes.
Helplessly,
I delved in the rivers of past lyric,
Hoping that its waters
Will wipe out my pain*

Night Time

It all started with many empty nights,
Unfulfilled dreams and broken promises.
It all started many winters ago,
With long rainy and snowy days
It all started with many foggy nights,
Deserted streets and undressed trees
It all started when nature,
My most precious companion,
Went on strike turning its sunshine
Into clouds.
Clouds, clouds, clouds all over
Hiding a persistent sun
Struggling to show its brilliance.
Clouds, clouds, clouds all over
Obscuring a bright star
Striving to save the night.

Where does time go?
The time when you were the idol
And the light of your people;
The time when everyone bowed
At the mere mention of your name.
Already, there are other hymns, other rhythms.
Where does time go?
The time when you shed your blood
Fighting for those cursed people.
Already, you are tossed aside!
Today, here you are, in a highland lying incognito, away from the sun,
All your dreams smashed at your feet.

Where have gone the smiles of my past?
They have evaporated
leaving me heartbroken.
Where have gone the hopes of my past?
They are stuck in time,
leaving me shriveling
While the cloth of despair drapes me.

*Coming from afar,
The beat of Tam-Tam,
Thunder crashing,
Unbridled spasm
Throughout my body.
Who am I?
Who have I become?*

Night Time

*Trapped in the bodies
Of warriors,
Forced to fight
A battle
That is not their own,
Kindred spirits
Crave to unburden
Their souls.*

Untainted dress
Traded for blood stained gown.
Sacrificial lamb
Served at the table
Of the uncanny.

Night Time

*Streams of blood
Running wild
Across the river of humanity.
Under the bridges of despair:
Distorted visions,
Shattered dreams,
Innocence turned
Upside down.*

Sara DeGraff

*In the firmament, it is foggy.
Out there in the wilderness,
It is hide and seek.
At the crossroad,
It is love.
In my heart,
It is downpour.
The secret of the nighttimes
Of my life.*

Night Time

In my hours of solitude,
I confide in the many quiet waters
Of the Universe.
In my hours of melancholy,
I long for a time
When the sun and the stars will shine
A time,
When my music mingling
With the singing of the birds
Will announce dawn.

Sara DeGraff

*Chanting hearts,
Bonding souls
Opening doorways.
Tolling bells,
Fading dreams,
Wandering hearts,
Floating souls.*

*The angry Gods
Have turned my body
Into a horse to gallop
Into forbidden alleys.
The Goddess of love
Has tied my hands
And opened
My love garden
For malicious
And mocking souls to come
And let their hair down
Some powerful forces
Are playing chess with my life.*

*This is not my home
My home is a castle
Built on top of a mountain,
Overlooking down below
Giving access to
Only a chosen few
This is not my garden!
In my garden,
Sunflowers and Moonflowers
Grow side by side
This is not my face!
Who is this Caricature
Frowning at me in the mirror?
This is not my music!
I've never played those notes before,
I've never danced to that tune before.
This is not my life!
Everything looks so
Unfamiliar
This is not my journey*

Night Time • 21

*Somewhere along the way
I might have gotten
lost*

*Time is as long as eternity
And eternity is on my side,
For eternity is nothing
But that boundless space
Where the now,
The yesterdays,
And tomorrow
Are just one.*

Night Time • 23

I remember a little spring
From the birthplace of my mother.
I remember the birds singing at dawn
While drinking from its elixir.
I remember its generosity
To dead leaves trying to revive themselves
From its sprightly water.
I remember seating under a mapou tree
Envying its freshness.
I remember its music always clear and joyful
Will I ever hear its song again?
Or have we parted never to meet again ?

*In the wilderness of my life:
The occasional twittering of the birds,
The inquisitive look of a deer,
The curiosity of a squirrel
Knocking gently at my door,
The soothing effect of a hot afternoon
By the lake,
The giganticness of the trees
Dressed for the festivities of summertime.
I stand disarmed!*

*It was only yesterday,
The Springtime of my life,
I moved into that temple.
Spring lasted but one morning!
Soon celebration for summertime began:
Dances to the sound of drums
Parades to the sound of trumpets,
long promenades,
Intermittent escapades.
The summertime of my life,
A festive time, indeed!
Soon I grew tired and fell asleep
In the arms of Morpheus.
Then, one afternoon,
The cold breeze of Autumn awoke me.
Not much time before Winter
Knocks at the door of my temple
Will I be ready?*

*I would like to be
A butterfly,
Fly from flower to flower
And surprise happiness.
I would like to be
Free as the wind,
And quicken nature.
I would like to be
Clear as daylight,
My little bird,
And be loved
As I am.*

Night Time •27

*The rambling of my spirit
Often makes me feel unsettled.
The unsettling nature of my heart
Sometimes makes me wander.
The wandering aspect of my journey
Often makes it impossible
For me to stand still.*

Sara DeGraff

I live in a hidden world
Never traveled by many,
A world surrounded
By trees of unknown
I travel through
Bumpy roads and wild rivers
Roads only seen
And rivers only crossed by a few
Throughout my pilgrimage
My suitcase amassed dust
Dirt got stuck to my shoes of
Greatness
And made my steps heavy-laden
Throughout my journey
I traveled through roads
Only dreamt by many

Night Time

*I see people
At the end of their journey
Cursing at
life's broken promises,
Advertising frauds
And misleading signposts.*

*I see people going to their Maker,
Exhausted and disappointed at the sum
Of their life's accomplishments.
I see newborns being welcomed
With symphonies and fanfares,
Exiting unnoticed at the end
Of their journey.
I see people born inconspicuous
Turning into the greatest teachers of our times
And living forever in our mind.
Are those being welcomed
With symphonies and fanfares
At the beginning of their journey
Really at the end of their glory?*

*World of clashed ideologies:
Destruction and fear
World of erroneous beliefs:
Piles of bones on the altar of humanity.*

Night Time

*lonely hearts searched
For each other in the dark
And there was no child.
No one to honor thy name
No one to carry our torch
No one to tell our tales
Our children are dying
No one to hail our ancestors
No one to lay us asleep
No one to carry our legacy
Our children are dying
Another starless night
lonely hearts searched
For each other in the dark
And there was no child.*

Sara DeGraff

Hope conquers all.
Hope delivers
From oppression
And domination.
Hope brings people together
In both times of brightness
And times of darkness.

Night Time

Here I am!
Standing at the doorway,
Between this world and beyond,
Hoping and Praying
That you will not cross over.

When you entered through
The portal of the mortal,
I guided your little steps.
Soon, they became giant ones
And took you to forbidden shores.
Why did you have to go there?
There were many roads
That you could have taken.
Why there?

Night Time

I've seen you walk away
Sacrificing a kiss
At the commissure of your lips
I've seen you walk away
An icy night of my life,
A demented surrender of my psyche.
I've seen you walk away,
Your retreat restrained my steps
The leash was my pain.

I am the bearer of life
I carry the children of the Universe
I am also their coach
If I do not train them well
They may be handicapped
For the duration of their journey
Sometimes, I admit my shoulders crumble
Under the magnitude of my assignment.

*I am the unsung hero,
I have unheard of prowess
And unshakable endurance.
I am an alchemist,
I transmute trapping waters
Into running waters
And transform deteriorating slums
Into safe heavens for little angels to fly
No matter how many betrayals,
I will not surrender.
I may fall but will not stay down.
I will always get up
So the show can go on.
My name is Woman.*

*My companion
Occasionally treats me
As a faded bouquet
And goes after burgeoning flowers
My children, after they get out of my carriage
Often walk away without looking back
Do not fear for me when you see me on the ground.
Do not fear for me when you see me convey my outcry to the world.
I am only articulating my dolor because I am wounded.*

love makes one cry
love makes one cruel
love makes one weak
love makes one whine
As soon as one opens her heart
It gets broken into tiny pieces.

*Away from you,
I feel lost and empty.
Inside my heart there is the frenziest tempest.
I tremble and mumble the melody of dizzy birds,
Hoping for a presage from a pilgrim dreamer.*

Night Time • 41

I am a quiet storm.
I am a warrior spirit
I am a pilgrim dreamer longing for bluer skies.
I am a leafless tree
Standing on an unrhythmical world.
I am a quiet storm.

All I've ever wanted
Was to travel with you a few miles.
All I've ever wanted was for you to awake me
In case I felt asleep and missed some scenes
All I've ever wanted was to look at life
through Your eyes.

*Happiness is somewhere
Playing hide and seek
The only way to catch it is to surprise it.*

Sara DeGraff

*I like wild flowers
Wild flowers are free-spirited,
Wild flowers are unpredictable,
Wild flowers are unruly,
Wild flowers are exciting.
I like wild flowers
Wild flowers turn me on,
Wild flowers make me feel.
Wild flowers make me want.*

Night Time •45

*Today I give myself to you.
Today I cease to be the isolated tree in the wilderness.
Both of us, we embark on the boat of life
Where our hearts linked forever,
Contemplate the beauty of the Spectacle.*

*Any day now,
The sky of my life will unravel.
Any day now,
I will reach the top of the mountain.
Thoughts and dreams about reaching the peak
Keep on coming to me.
Any day now!*

*Any day now,
I will find an unsurpassed peacefulness.
The waves from that lingering storm
Will transport me to a new horizon
Where the many quiet waters of the Universe
Will once again give my soul a restful
shoulder.*

Night Time • 47

*Forgive my trespasses
For I was senseless
It never occurred to me
That my missteps were disturbing
The rhythm of the Universe
I now understand that
To rid the world of its pains and discord
I must replace hatred with love
Anger with forgiveness
Isolation with togetherness.*

*Many songs to sing,
Many steps to take,
Many dreams to dream
Many discourses to make
Many ways to go
Many things to do
But one thing to remember
Together, you and I
Can make the world a better place.
You can make a small difference
I can make a small difference.*

*If only I had listened
To the irking whispers of my spirit
I would have taken a more enlightened path,
And you, the shadow of obscurity,
Would not have been able to withstand the light.*

I am light
You are darkness
I will illumine the dark areas of your being.
I will enter in your most remote places
I am light
You are darkness
And I will not rest until I transform you into light.

*The whole purpose of life:
The ongoing unveiling of truths.*

www.ingramcontent.com/pod-product-compliance
Lightning Source LLC
Chambersburg PA
CBHW050330010526
44119CB00050B/742